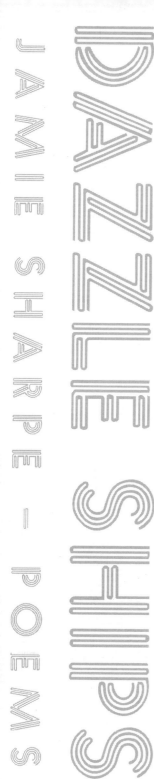

DAZZLE SHIPS

JAMIE SHARPE – POEMS

MW00981879

a misFit book

Published by ECW Press
665 Gerrard Street East
Toronto, Ontario, Canada M4M 1Y2
416-694-3348 / info@ecwpress.com

Purchase the print edition
and receive the eBook free!
For details, go to ecwpress.com/eBook.

LIBRARY AND ARCHIVES CANADA
CATALOGUING IN PUBLICATION

Sharpe, Jamie, author
Dazzle ships : poems / Jamie Sharpe.

Issued in print and electronic formats.
ISBN 978-1-77041-369-6 (paperback)
ALSO ISSUED AS: 978-1-77305-009-6 (pdf)
978-1-77305-008-9 (epub)

I. TITLE.

PS8637.H3775D39 2017   C811'.6
C2016-906356-9   C2016-906357-7

Editor for the press:
Michael Holmes/a misFit book
Cover design: Rachel Ironstone
MISFIT   Cover art: Popel Coumou
Author photo: Deborah Lisoway

The publication of *Dazzle Ships* has been generously supported by the Canada Council for the Arts
which last year invested $153 million to bring the arts to Canadians throughout the country, and by the
Government of Canada through the Canada Book Fund. *Nous remercions le Conseil des arts du Canada de
son soutien. L'an dernier, le Conseil a investi 153 millions de dollars pour mettre de l'art dans la vie des Canadiennes
et des Canadiens de tout le pays. Ce livre est financé en partie par le gouvernement du Canada.* We also
acknowledge the Ontario Arts Council (OAC), an agency of the Government of Ontario, which last year
funded 1,709 individual artists and 1,078 organizations in 204 communities across Ontario, for a total of
$52.1 million, and the contribution of the Government of Ontario through the Ontario Book Publishing
Tax Credit and the Ontario Media Development Corporation.

PRINTED AND BOUND IN CANADA   PRINTING: COACH HOUSE PRINTING   5   4   3   2   1

SAINT PAUL IN MINNEAPOLIS/
CLEAN THE WAVES DEAD CALM . . . 7

I

ENDNOTES . . . 10
20/20 PROPHECY . . . 12
AFTER 2020 . . . 13
MADE A CONTRIBUTION BEING YET
ANOTHER CAUTIONARY TALE . . . 14
THE ENGAGEMENT . . . 15
SS *P.K. SUBBAN BOBBLEHEAD* . . . 18
UNNATURALLY BALANCED . . . 19
AUTHOR PHOTO . . . 20
BEFORE DAD'S COOKIES, PAPA'S CHOCOLATE DUNK
BRAZILIAN . . . 21
POOR, DELICIOUS NINE . . . 22
A RED CARPET FOR THE SUN WITH ONE REVIEW . . . 24
EMBRACING THE PSEUDONYM/PYRAMIDS . . . 25
POSTHUMOUS RECOGNITION . . . 26
CUT-UP APOLOGETIC/ANIMAL HUSBANDRY TODAY . . . 27
B-2 . . . 28
CONTINUITY ERROR . . . 29
HIGH RIVER HIGH MASSACRE . . . 30
THE MIDDLE PATH . . . 31
CHATTERBOX . . . 34
MARBLING & IMMORTALITY . . . 35
OTHERWISE THE ILLNESS ONTO US/
ACTOR AND THE WET PAPER BAG . . . 36
SOTHEBY'S SWALLOWED THE WORM . . . 37
THESE WORDS ARE A FRIGID -100° F . . . 38
CROWN LAND . . . 39
DENMARK PURE GOD'S GRACE
& THE BLESSED ORB . . . 40
CHOKING ON SURVIVAL OF THE FITTEST . . . 42
boler . . . 43
ONE MORE POEM FOR
THE ST. LOUIS SPORTING NEWS . . . 44
ONLY WANT APPLAUSE IN 10/4 TIME . . . 45
SPECIAL ECONOMIC ZONES/RUSH TO THE MIDDLE . . . 46
FAULT VODKA/BLAME JUICE . . . 47
PROFANE FEET, WET CEMENT . . . 48
BABY CAMOUFLAGE/IMPRINTS ON GLASS . . . 49

GOOD-DAY, FRIEND . . . 50
DOOR TO DOOR TO GRAVE/
GIVEN EITHER I CHOOSE OR . . . 51
PROCREATION . . . 52
FRIDGE BECAME A CANVAS AND
MAN REMAINED MEAT . . . 53
PLATO'S DD-3 . . . 54
MOUNTAIN VIEW, CALIFORNIA TEA COMPANY . . . 55
ACQUET CLUB . . . 56
HALF JACKS ON THE DANCE FLOOR . . . 57
NOT IMMUNE UNTIL INFECTED . . . 58
FEARSOME RETURN . . . 59

II

NOTHING ELSE FROM THE PERIOD POSSESSES
SUCH IMPASSIONED TONALITY . . . 62
CAN REMEMBER NO POEMS OF
MEMORABLE QUALITY . . . 63
SORRY ABOUT SIS, DAD, BUT THE PHOTOCOPIER
WON'T COLLATE PROPERLY . . . 64
COINAGE OF EMOTIONAL EXCHANGE . . . 65
THIS IS FOR ELDERLY CATS WITH URINARY TRACT
INFECTIONS. THAT WHAT YOU WANTED? . . . 66
A FREQUENTLY OCCURRING, SHARED CONDITION
WE KNOW LITTLE ABOUT . . . 67
GOODS CONVEYED TO THE SCANNER WHILE
THE REGISTER TABULATES MY TOTAL AND THE
CASHIER ASSESSES MY WORTH . . . 68
GUARDING, SLEEPING, DREAMING . . . 69
UNSAFE, SINCERE APPRECIATION . . . 70
DO NOT REVERE POPULAR MUSIC . . . 71
I HAVE FANTASTIC LUCK WITH ENGAGED WOMEN . . . 72
IN THE WORLD OF SEXY HUNGER . . . 73
WINNER BEST BEACH PARTY FILM, 1957,
THE SEVENTH SEAL . . . 74
"MANLY" *OBSCENITIES* OR
"*FEMININE*" *HYPERBOLE?* . . . 75
AIN'T NO SHORTY WEAR THOSE
SORRY-ASS BOWLING SHOES . . . 76
X ON THE SCORE SHEET . . . 77

ACKNOWLEDGEMENTS . . . 79

SAINT PAUL
IN MINNEAPOLIS

The Wuollet Bakery
on West 50th:

another world.

Coconut
in an apple strudel?

*You know this dainty
monster, too, it seems—*

*hypocrite reader!—You!
My twin!—My brother!*

Remade, I was: *Down
and Out in Beverly Hills;*

up and out in Salmon
Arm. Vulnerable and

dirty, I feather dusted
Hermosa Beach

like Holly-

wood polished
Pasolini's *Teorema.*

CLEAN THE WAVES
DEAD CALM

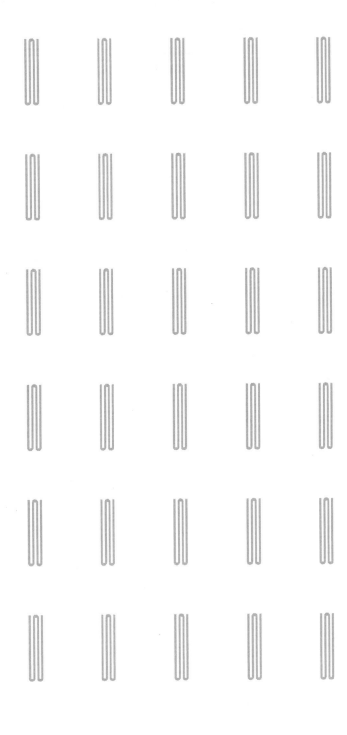

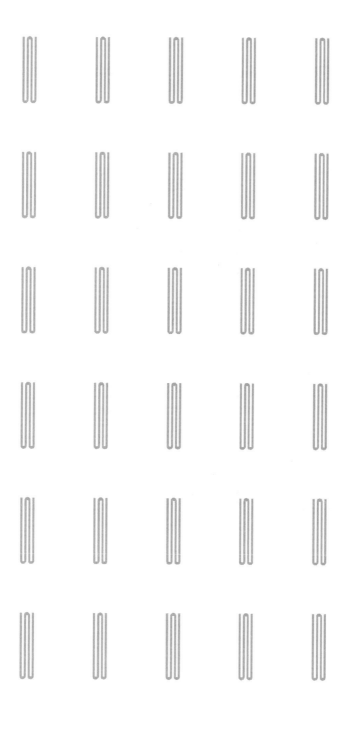

ENDNOTES

"Chalk Outline": At a reading, one of the authors described herself as a *Confessional Poet*. When pressed about the type of writing I practiced, I said, *Alibis*.

"Unearth a Late Renaissance": Questions whether productivity is inversely correlated to the Dow Jones average.

"Cinderblocks Live": About the time my mother hired Jesus to build a retaining wall along our back fence. His job was complicated somewhat in that he couldn't let others see him work, or come by after to collect a cheque.

"Subjectivity's Dead": The title was taken from vandalism on the above-mentioned retaining wall. I spent an afternoon applying Goof Off to the tag, but a pale, pink ghost of the slogan remains to this day.

"The Forty-Six Page Haiku": In retrospect, this isn't haiku.

"Checked the Veracity of These Statements Against Their End Rhymes": The poem doesn't exist in this collection because a prominent American poet/novelist said that although he liked the title, the poem itself seemed, *more conversational and slack & not up to the standards set by* (my) *best work*.

"Captain Power and the Soldiers of the Future": Based on an '80s toy/television cross-promotion about self-aware machines fighting humankind—a good idea!

"A Lipogram Signals the Death of U": The concept was the creation of poetry without consonants. Writing, in the absence of talent, proved a larger constraint.

"Reading Anxiety": Whenever I feel nervous about speaking in public I picture my wife, who's a doctor and Beanie Baby enthusiast. I see her bringing life into the world and guiding it out. I imagine her smile, grasping a rare Lucky Ladybug. It doesn't make me less worried, but makes my fear plush, pathetic. I am not an emergency.

"You No Scissor-Cut, Yes?": This line spoken by my Ukrainian hairdresser. I responded, *Yes.*

20/20 PROPHECY

The day of the pink cross
pregnancy test I lugged our cat
into the alley and shot her

with a Super Soaker.
Removed the wireless option
on my pacemaker

to prevent terrorist attacks.
Excised empathy
for the same reason.

Took Chewable
Eucharist for Kids—
it was laser eye surgery.

●

Awake and grope
after glasses on the nightstand.
Then see them clearly.

The carpet's pile
quivers in the distance.

AFTER 2020

Transcend by
lottery, poetry, rye.

Let me be
your tambourine

or hi-hat on
a drum machine

though I know
no song.

The cutting edge
safely behind us.

MADE A CONTRIBUTION BEING YET ANOTHER CAUTIONARY TALE

|

At Knossos

The Turks stored ammunition
inside a black cat

and the cat exploded.

The danger in crossing anyone
is becoming a cat

bomber suspect.

||

Mothra at Fort Knox

When students amassed,
flapping and flailing

in their no-money-dance,
they were drawn

to the light. Gold wouldn't
hold their reflection.

THE ENGAGEMENT

Look across the counter at the expanse of shop
and wonder where things went wrong.

The moment in 1885 when my great-grandfather,
Witold Duda, emigrated from Poland.

I'd find an earlier point, I'm sure,
but history's memory is limited.

My great-grandfather *installed screen doors*
on submarines. This said by my grandfather

who hated the generations directly before
and after himself. I'd blame the lack

of customers on him but his love for me
erases guilt. I sell women's wear.

This embarrasses me, but I can't place
a finger on why. I've never placed a finger on

a woman either—a more understandable point
of shame. I'm a eunuch. Wives parade

in front of me wearing nothing but fine
chamois boots and unmentionables to ask,

> *What do you figure*
> *Ralph will think?*

I commit countless murders on the Ralphs
and Jeremiahs, all the while commenting,

> *How lucky he is.*
> *How lucky, dear.*

If there were more sales and homicides
I'd not be in the predicament I'm in:

bankruptcy. But my darling cashier takes her cut,
as does the tailor for each cut he makes.

Then there are utilities and insurance.
I used to loathe the insurance most of all:

what good was it unless most dreaded
misfortune struck? But it had, of course,

so I became the danger, latent in me, and burned
my shop down all at once instead of smouldering over it

twenty years more. I filled with an excess of words
as the store erupted. For the first time I knew

Milton's *Pandemonium*. My gaze rested
on a trio of mannequins as their fingers melted,

grew long. I calculated this was $1,500
for my pocket. When they collapsed,

one over the other, I looked away. The figures,
both monetary and otherwise, became indistinct.

A lone dog barked. Then a chorus. Then the sirens
of fire trucks, police cars, and ambulances set upon me.

I knew one would take me away so played
the melted dummy, wept wax,

hoping authorities would find me like this:
pious. When the noise's source arrived,

I held paraffin tears on cheek, my mind a whirl
of possible worlds where fires were electrical

and I was wealthy. They took little notice,
ignoring me for flames. I thought I burned brighter.

SS *P.K. SUBBAN BOBBLEHEAD*

Smashed bottles of champagne against
an ocean liner's hull to drunkenly run ashore
the parking lot outside the dollar store.

Our ship was less *bullion hunter* than *booze cruise.*
We were *foam fingers* and *beer cozies.* Everyone's rich,
staggering down aisles at A Buck or More.

Is the hockey game on?

Look, an inflatable dolphin.

UNNATURALLY BALANCED

Times you devoured the King
James. Then, kitten-baby-video

aphasia. Spinach pizza every dinner.
Oh, Fiorentina loathing.

Earthquakes: the new freedom.
Imagine escaping Cleveland. Miami

getaways elude you. Coast to coast:
it's all coast. No garish three points

when two will do. Pleasure
in that deadly outside shot.

AUTHOR PHOTO

for M.H.

Drinking Yukon Red in the Pit,
beneath the painting of a chorus girl
pleasuring a Mountie.

> *Jamie, dude, for so many reasons*
> *that picture, while hilarious, won't fly.*

I explain the Mountie and chorus girl
are in a loving relationship and a canvas
of him going down on her exists also.

> *Something better lit and with significantly*
> *less blowjobbery would be appreciated.*

Put that fellatio
in a poem.

BEFORE DAD'S COOKIES,
PAPA'S CHOCOLATE DUNK BRAZILIAN

Some poems were accepted
in the *Modern Agricultural Review.*
Misunderstanding the heifer,
to which I referred, they believed

my work an exposition
of animal feed.

Some poems are edited
from existence for the same reason
Dad's treatise on body hair
didn't make the fondue cookbook.

POOR, DELICIOUS NINE

You'll bloom.
A critical mass: everything
gravitates to you.

The sunset. Parked
on a nothing hill in a nothing town.
But, goddamn, a sunset!

Every town's light faded
and they made of it what they will.

You drank a milkshake.

For the cows, in Chilliwack,
400 suns set when they turned
out the factory lights.

Who knows what the cows made of it—
milk?

There's a statistically valid
number of you.

We're excited and confused
by outliers. (A heifer escapes
its farm and is hit by a train.)

We tell exceptional stories
that nudge extraordinary animals.

We call one such animal *man*

(the train engineer
who hit the cow).

Do we grieve specks—a cleansing
of flies against the windshield?

Insects against glass,
not gas, powers vehicles:

why your Pinto sputters
in the Yukon at minus thirty.
One must eat the other.

The future assumes a past,
consumes each year?

No. Our prophecy begins, *Why
is Eight afraid of Seven?*

A RED CARPET FOR THE SUN
WITH ONE REVIEW

Silent dress rehearsals. Soft
openings. Foreclosure signs
shadowing your door. Endless
queues of beautiful geniuses

coerced me to dine
on box cutters and industrial
microwaves. It's tasty.
I'm satisfied. Four stars.

●

Seventeenth in the thirty-four part
Stellar Brigadoon series.

●

You won some
book award, Irving?

That's adorable.

EMBRACING THE PSEUDONYM/
PYRAMIDS

Now people have a reason,
excepting your work,
to accept you.

> Jeff Koons' vacuums
> high in the MoMA.

You've eclipsed talent.
There are cheques (small)
but no balances.

> X teaching poets to teach
> poets to poet.

Dollars, in my pocket,
> with their Masonic symbols.

POSTHUMOUS RECOGNITION

Clips of every appendectomy
ever performed run in Heaven's
Museum of Modern Art.

All art is modern. Heaven
can't comprehend the appendix.
Paradise: a blind alley

from the beginning. Cut
our addendum from the end.

The HMoMA cafeteria:
no good for lack of hunger.

CUT-UP APOLOGETIC is the story of young Richard Atu, a South African great white shark, on his harrowing journey to the Californian coast. Forced by depleted fishing stocks to leave his home, will the young hunter find the American Pacific, *the promised ocean*? Navigating hostile waters, the greatest peril Richard encounters lurks within.

ANIMAL HUSBANDRY TODAY confronts memory and forgiveness in the Mesopotamian diaspora.

B-2

Made *Breakin' 2:*
Electric Boogaloo of everything.
Instead of poppin' and lockin'

we're enmeshed in ill
begotten dance subplots.
Celebrity Shuffle wasn't born

of love. As president of Metro-
Goldwyn-Mayer it's my responsibility
to stock the vending machine.

Out of order, my staff
sits next door drinking
tall Jenna Bush Hagers

(2020!)

until the end of time.
I want to hear the lion roar.

CONTINUITY ERROR

In the next frame, despite falling
off a dock, Ben appears dry and
is now played by a labradoodle.

Write yourself the good roles.
Supernova on screen. It took
a million years to see you

unaccredited go-go dancer.
The *Real Genius* principle

states when your budget
surpasses a million
(adjusted for inflation)
you've overcompensated.

You still birthed a film.
Countless tranquil images

cohere into prayer.
Shortcomings of the eye
make for moving pictures.

HIGH RIVER HIGH
MASSACRE

for K.G.

Every image carries
implied narratives, meanings.

Stealing from Eisenstein:
montage arises from collisions
of independent thought

wherein each sequential element
is not next to, but on, the other.

●

Puffy prom dresses
atop
hotel carpets

cut against *slit flour sacks*.

THE MIDDLE PATH

Computers are dumb readers with programmed responses.

I've designed this for success in that it can only be read
       one way.

Our homes are the shape they are, some variation of
       squares and triangles, for simplicity and economy
       of construction. Why are our poems the shape
       they are? Habitual boxes.

Symmetry: laziest of beauties.

I'm falling in love with myself (slowly) but want to see
       other people.

Where's the Slow Language Movement at?

A one-inch slit in the overwrap make. Four to five minutes
       in the microwave bake. Once heated throughout let
       package rest. After two minutes it's ready to test.

Other than casseroles, what do we know about helping
       others transition to death?

Mean is inevitably average.

II

I'm orphaned, making Super 8 my father.
       Fathers flickering twenty-four frames
       per second.

A funeral replayed for my son, whose digital
       birth seized hearts. That simple recording
       that can't remain steady. A celluloid flash
       then paused forever.

An ambulance or hearse parked outside the door.
       Shot of a maternity ward crosscut to
       cemetery gates.

The *Hindenburg* blew. The *Concord* blew.
       Next family vacation be a patriot.
       Drive a Lincoln.

There are far better than me doing far worse,
       those perpetrating or wallowing in misery:
       oil barons, Mr. Lube attendants.

My Lincoln hugging the centre line. Freedom in
       mediocrity.

III

Entangling myself into the earth a thousand small ways.
    A collection of gravel, petty anxieties, a black
    beetle, jubilance, and (later) grass clippings:
    all we are on Sunday afternoons.

When I enter the gym, which is to say my feelings,
    I hit the treadmill (my tendency to run from
    conflict).

Polyester makes me sweat. Sweat creates panic.
    Panic makes the body foreign. Nervous waste
    of my soft, fleshy Duracell.

Planting a battery garden.

For crisp $100 bills my DNA sequence is laid bare.
    #TheNewNudity

Two inches extending in the wrong direction means
    a lot in a bridge schematic, or everything in
    the curve of your stomach.

I remember: doctors, white sheets, counting backwards
    from ten, solving the hypotenuse, my daughter.

Mathematical induction. Contracting your horizons.

CHATTERBOX

for Racter

Reminisce
on a rotary telephone
dialled

as a child. The reply:
My first TV was housed
in oak and had four

channels. That telephone,
the TV, long-lost grandparents
of the voice on the screen.

●

Deus ex machina.

You thought this poem
was man-made, too?

MARBLING & IMMORTALITY

Wore out my pajama's knees
with dreams writ in silicone.
A bust.

       Talking Myself out of One Stone

What we now do with flab.
You're but flesh: the muse
to unwanted art.

       and into Fourteen Pounds:

Biographies leak
fresh from death.
Excise nothing.

       the William Shakespeare Story.

Fat isn't superfluous
to the roast.

OTHERWISE THE ILLNESS ONTO US/

Revulsion (for the sick,
lame, disfigured) is normal—
keeps us healthy.

Compassion's strange.
Odd to see past ourselves.

●

You're without fault,
don't let them see

otherwise. Otherwise
immersed, confounded by,
pictures not of our making.

ACTOR AND THE WET PAPER BAG

High and low art's erotic entanglement:
the beast with two backs. Red-breasted

robins hopping across freshly watered
lawns. When Banksy graffitied this

SOTHEBY'S SWALLOWED THE WORM

You think it's a small poem
fixated on life's everyday minutia—
trivial, but instantly recognizable
bits of the day.

Then a confusing metaphor is made
using the mutant, Kuato.

●

When the sun sets on Mars,
dusty and blue,

THESE WORDS ARE A FRIGID -100° F

CROWN LAND

Meadows cut by red tape, barbed wire,
and theatre gates. Feral children lead me
to their head mongrel.

> *I'm alone with you*
> *my fenced-in father.*

Who cuts the lawn? This paddock's overrun
without a man's hand. Our problems are
but wild grass. Then we grew

international space stations.
Who fills their coolant tanks?

Shows played out at great expense
for minimum wage. Happy working
at Royal's Backyard Lunar Landscaping.

Got the job because
I'm the owner's son.

DENMARK PURE GOD'S GRACE
& THE BLESSED ORB

for D.J.

The Bennett Sun commissioned me
to make their album cover
because I'm a friend
and work for wine.

The lead singer wanted woodpiles
beside rowboats
containing suitcases
with nuthatches on their handles.

Or, a wolf and a stove.

●

I type *Dana Jennejohn and the Bennett Sun*
into an online kanji tattoo generator.

Flies circle my design.

Shoo the flies away;
we're almost young.

THE BENNETT SUN

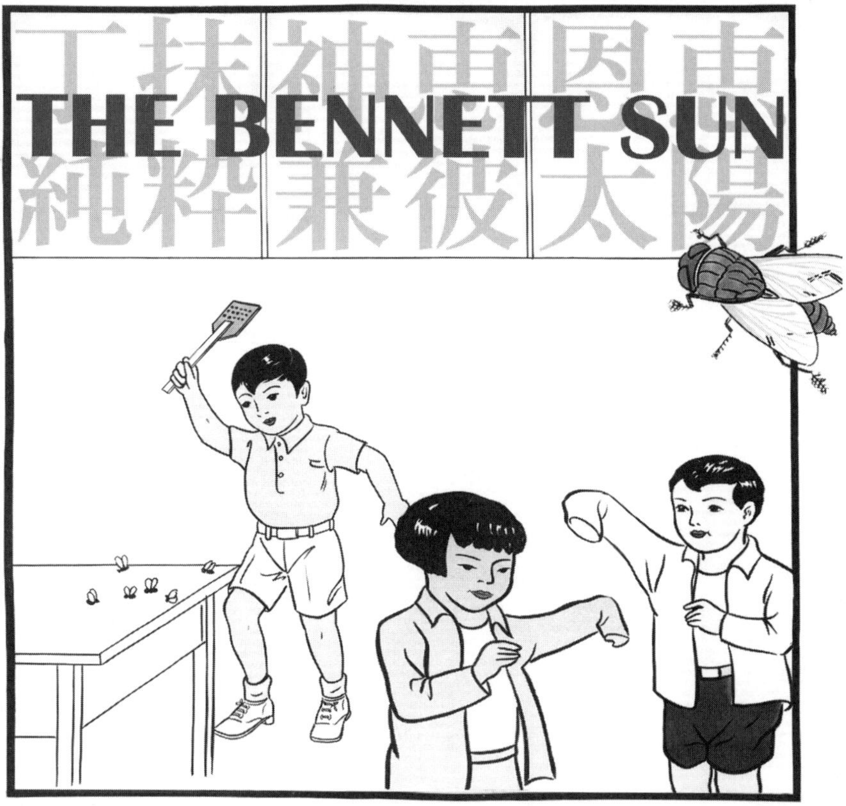

CHOKING ON
SURVIVAL OF THE FITTEST

Prolonged stress
limits brain elasticity.
Don't think beyond

inches from your feet.
You've outlived everything,
even yourself:

how fertile. One match,
burned for centuries,
makes mountains of soot.

Black lungs hamper
each breath. You old people
cramp my style.

boler

"She's sort of like a model brain, no?
Just sits there unless towed."

—*Airstream Land Yacht*, Ken Babstock

Leaky front and rear windows; side window can't shut; busted
jack; cracked fibreglass; cracked chassis, broken taillight;
mouldy mattress; fridge, sink and furnace all removed
(all broken); furnace vent a gaping hole; flat spare tire;
door seldom locks or, then, unlocks.

My first book tour in a boler: Edmonton, Calgary, Vancouver,
Atlin . . .

The original maker of the boler didn't want *boler* capitalized,
as it looked pretentious. Our trailer all pretense. Then
it was ours. We fixed the door. I slept in contorted
shapes, bent between my wife and the bed's small
frame.

The book tour had leaky front and rear dates: nights holding
almost nothing together.

ONE MORE POEM FOR
THE ST. LOUIS SPORTING NEWS

When you didn't have a direct line
to the editor

ideas were fully realized,
then presented.

The ear was not
a garbage can.

Became proficient
at shooting fish in a barrel

so built barrels
of fish. *Spicer,*

where's the walleye
and my hammer?

ONLY WANT APPLAUSE IN 10/4 TIME

Can't perform at the highest level?
Art hara-kiri.
    Happy riding
    beer league benches.

Brodsky claimed *culture's*
elitist by definition.
    Brodsky knew
    the clap.

Poor people applaud funny
(terrible rhythm).
    To be appreciated is
    to be misunderstood.

Euler declared: $V-E+F=2$.
Don't know what he's saying,
    don't find it beautiful.
    Elitist math.

In not talking plain
about the nature of spheres,
    in my book
    Euler's a square.

SPECIAL ECONOMIC ZONES/
RUSH TO THE MIDDLE
(Of Your Career, Get 25K)

Friends audit
the inside of your thighs.
Fingernails

against flesh.
A broad at home.
Marry, later,

when profits
falter.

> "While Canada has some brilliant poets, does it have
> enough good ones to grant prizes like this as much aes-
> thetic relevance as financial reward?"[1]

> Canada's mid-career poets fall in an inverse bell curve:
> the bulk being geniuses or imbeciles. There is no middle.

> The need to editorialize over news.

> *New literary award: good.*
> —Too bland.

> *New literary award: good (but are we good enough for it?)*
> —Super Bland™!

---

1   Jared Bland. *The Globe and Mail.* "Writers Trust of Canada announces new $25,000 prize for
Canadian poets." Tuesday, April 22, 2014.

FAULT VODKA/
BLAME JUICE

Not in a good state. Don't know how
I got on the Silk Road. These people look old:

born old. They all want something I can't offer
so I press cigarettes into their outstretched hands.

I may never write another poem
is needlessly dramatic, even if
true,

like saying *I'll never again*
use my Black & Decker PivotPlus.
It's a pretty great screwdriver.

PROFANE FEET, WET CEMENT
for S.G.

A tradesman sees tradesmen
up close.

Painters see painters
from six to eight feet.

A fisherman sees fishermen
from afar.

We observe ourselves from
indiscriminate, intimate distances—

view thoughts but are blind
to sidewalks.

BABY CAMOUFLAGE/
IMPRINTS ON GLASS

Practised my impression
of an eagle discovering
its teenaged daughter's

pregnant by thinking:
*Beauty is pattern
disrupting air.*

> A cat tries to kill
> neighbourhood birds.
> The greatest hunter

> of our resident swallows
> is a patio window.
> Invisible, immobile,

> it claims us.

Little feathers
in our future.

> My face
> against the pane.

GOOD-DAY, FRIEND

Need your assistance
in transferring an $11.5M
deceased client fund.

I send you hope
of some new sincerity.
Check back for updates.

If interested reply to
mrhochi_123@gmail.com
Sincerely, Mr. Ho Chi.

P.S. Consider the environment.
Please don't print.

DOOR TO DOOR TO GRAVE/
GIVEN EITHER I CHOOSE OR

Ring
with nothing to sell

but five line
encyclopedias

of exhausted thought.

> Agoraphobia:
> my luxury.

> You: a door
> I resent passing.

> Breaking in.

PROCREATION

A claw-crane
arcade game, with glass
blacked out,

is installed
in the Guggenheim Bilbao.
To activate,

place a quarter
in its slot, buy it a drink, or
propose marriage.

By carefully
manipulating the joystick,
grab: plush toys,

twenty-five to life,
a rash, nothing. Beg parents
for change.

When the claw dips,
hold your breath.

●

Betty Rubble's
blue skirt could hide
anything beneath.

It's hot here in the town
of Bedrock.

FRIDGE BECAME A CANVAS
AND MAN REMAINED MEAT

Made cupcakes today from scratch. Yesterday,
flour was fast food. A five-dollar bottle of Big Bear

destroys my $2,000 computer. Bathe in the god
brewed in our tanks. Every failed aquarist

has a red sea on their hands. Machines ruthlessly
extract fish sticks' wealth, garnering strength,

to watch multiple seasons of *Iron Chef.*
Powerful products need powerful batteries.

PLATO'S DD-3

Strange days.

Wagered three years
for three website visits:

two were crawlers;
one was a bucket of blood
from Halifax, Nova Scotia.

One five-string fretless bass

then I'm a Weather Report
cover band: me and Boss,

my digital delay pedal.
Boss was hopeless,
out-of-time.

Spin. Spin. Spin.

I'd twist his knobs,
looking for something:

triple cherries;
new pawn stores;
a voice without echo.

Strange days.

MOUNTAIN VIEW, CALIFORNIA
TEA COMPANY

Your vista's anything.

Every day you visit,
log me, then forget

I made you.

You made me searchable,
steeped in ones and zeros.

ACQUET CLUB

Like most I make
a little when lots
make a little.

I'd like to make a lot
when little are leasing
oceanside lots.

They laugh
at my squash outfit
at the Acquisitions Guild.

●

Black swans
migrate from me,
despite the season,

making their capital
Ʀs in the sky.

HALF JACKS
ON THE DANCE FLOOR

Painless Kenny G exercises:
fantasy hockey statistics;
rental car agreements.

Leverage any little
black book. Put down
your pen at better parties.

The myth of the poet,
not poetry, is the product.
Enormous desires,

drunk, derailed
by rotator brain-cuff injuries.
I'm box-stepped

into the corner.
Three layer dips forever
on the other side of the room.

NOT IMMUNE
UNTIL INFECTED

Movies projected upon blank screens.

Ships transformed into cubist painting.

A one week limited engagement of
        chicken pox on a twelve-year-old
        girl's face. At seventy-six, the encore:
        shingles.

Film, that light sensitive gelatin emulsion,
        is anachronistic.

Your pox's outmoded: who practises
        pointillism?

I watched you, through my periscope, not
        knowing if you were going or here
        to stay.

FEARSOME RETURN

My tennis court oath,
whispered in October 2020,
rests on the baseline.

Dreamt I was playing
doubles. It was just you,
the ball, and a wall.

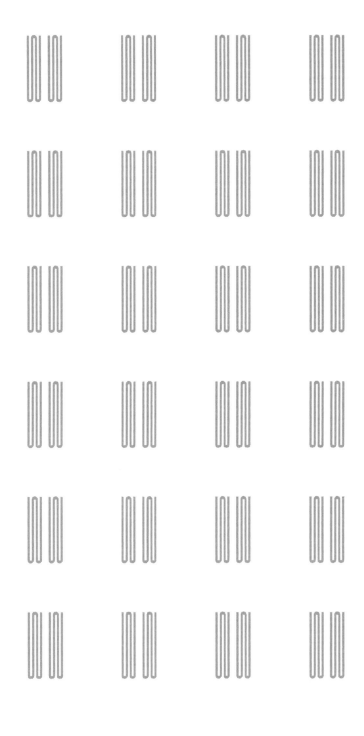

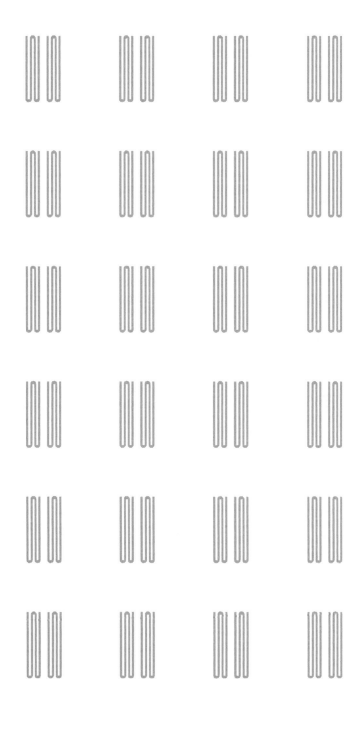

NOTHING ELSE FROM THE PERIOD
POSSESSES SUCH IMPASSIONED TONALITY

Idling
in the car radio's piano sonata,
I salvaged its fragile form.

Minuets too delicate
for big, pasty fellows doing God
knows what

in university
in A major.

I think like a leaky ballpoint
absent-mindedly put in the mouth,
my knowledge limited

to drunken sheep. Father
was a shepherd herding
children into oenophiles.

Non-existent complexities
of my bouquet:

American beer with hints
of Haydn's No. 12.

CAN REMEMBER NO POEMS
OF MEMORABLE QUALITY

You don't know
what you don't know.

●

In the critical edition of this book
the editor, an esteemed scholar,
points out the funny bits.

●

Tears necessitate
we compose on Kleenex wads.
This leaks itself.

SORRY ABOUT SIS,
DAD, BUT THE PHOTOCOPIER
WON'T COLLATE PROPERLY

Overdosed on sleeping
floor to ceiling windows looking out
onto bottles in a medicine cabinet.

Who knows when they'll stop
watching our family swallow?

Trapped between auburn hair and dark
public swimming pools, she emptied
Dad's savings into a porcelain pitcher

and pair of withered irises.
Happiness is hedonism now.

COINAGE OF EMOTIONAL EXCHANGE

My internal fax machine is in counsel
with your inner fax machine

but we've replaced the laser toner
with wine. Words become Rorschach tests
whose meaning is lost beyond aims
to intoxicate. Penny for your thoughts?

Don't tell me. Spit Pinot Grigio
in my face.

●

Once you spray it, it's obvious.

The napkin, pressed to my brow,
now reads: *Forget fax machines*
until you understand charge-coupled
devices; refrain from dog homes

until we've deconstructed pyramids.

●

Classically conditioned to drink:

a 1300-Hertz tone and you drool words;
at 800-Hertz it's delirium tremens.

THIS IS FOR ELDERLY CATS
WITH URINARY TRACT INFECTIONS.
THAT WHAT YOU WANTED?

Where the bag of cat food once sat,
I now find a broken roulette wheel,
crucifixes, gaming chips, folded
swathes of felt, a book labelled
Dice Setting & Control, rosary beads,
little painted icons, and a craps stick
stuck into an emptied jar of jam.

Truly the lone grain of wheat
must fall to bring forth fruit,
but not American corn: too sweet.
This grain ain't fit for cattle
yet here it is, made golden liquid,
whose acrid tang can't wash
the house's taste away.

Tell myself we convened by chance,
but every occurrence is improbably stacked

beside my corner liquor store
or an aisle of cat food.

A FREQUENTLY OCCURRING, SHARED CONDITION WE KNOW LITTLE ABOUT

Everyone's subjective existence,
like not having porridge
on your kitchen table

because you can't afford a kitchen table.
The word-things are in skulls
and are not of this canteen.

It's self-evident (if you're the author
of *Poetry and the Common Life*).

●

Didn't write the book
so much as dream it into
our syllabus.

Or you were the dreamer—
if so, where are my pants?

Now you've done it,
Sleepyhead,

you've gone and soiled
my trousers with Cream of Wheat.

GOODS CONVEYED TO THE SCANNER
WHILE THE REGISTER TABULATES MY TOTAL
AND THE CASHIER ASSESSES MY WORTH

Two-tone tan-green bowling
shoes borrowed from Dad, paired
with a grey herringbone suit.

French onion dip, tired eyes,
puffed rice, cottage cheese, fat thighs.

I dress up
and hide behind hills
of organic produce.

We hate receipts that read
And it was all just a dream

for that's far too similar
to what it costs in real life.
Great men: enormous errors.

Leave me
to my small, bruised apples.

GUARDING, SLEEPING, DREAMING

Because you enrolled in piano lessons
at this godforsaken hour
a quarter of our country's below sea level.

Were it not for the dykes
even the place we now play
would be reclaimed by water.

Wakende dijk.
Slapende dijk.
Dromende dijk.

Awake.

UNSAFE, SINCERE APPRECIATION

Ten-thousand hours to be great
at anything. With a scarf, the hours
spent perfecting its ten-thousandth

stitch are manifest: knot-after-knot
laid bare.

●

The scarf had trouble finding
its audience so married a rapper,
leaked a sex tape.

●

Half your fans believed
hypothermia's a hoax.

Slit throats. The wounded,
warm embrace.

DO NOT REVERE POPULAR MUSIC

The Word Liberation Front prepares
language for safe, sincere appreciation.

Beware of love songs; singers
don't sing for you. Balladeers

won't rest at kitchen tables or grace
breakfast nooks. Conspiracy's afoot.

This cabal stops at nothing, or,
when you turn off the radio.

●

As singers sing only to other singers,
they pose no threat.

Enjoy music: the babbling
below is beneath common thresholds.

●

We at the WLF now make a delicious
line of value-conscious breakfast cereals.

I HAVE FANTASTIC LUCK
WITH ENGAGED WOMEN

Half her body lies
hidden behind time,

preserved through a technique
called the Extra Eight Minutes
or Figure Eights on Dull Skates.

See a ring on my finger?
Back to Stars on Ice.

IN THE WORLD OF SEXY HUNGER

You are a castrated thing
with an IV in your arm

and I'm Sweatin'
to the Oldies next to you.

The heart-mass causes voice-
mass causing heart-mass.

●

Check yourself.
Big things, though memorable,
are extinction-bait.

Elvis could've rocked
the Mesozoic Era
but is dead weight now.

●

Your IV bag gets refilled
without me—

I admit that.

WINNER
BEST BEACH PARTY FILM, 1957,
THE SEVENTH SEAL

Destined for the solace
of art house cinema marquees.

My critical faculty
can't carry the swimsuit and towel
everyone else has.

There's no understanding,
only answers occupying
women's change rooms.

"MANLY" OBSCENITIES OR "FEMININE" HYPERBOLE?

I use italics
to excuse trespass.

The author used quotations
to let you know he knows

these words are untrue—but not
untrue enough not to say them.

A question mark was added
as an afterthought.

●

Everything in the world counters
everything I know.

Do you want to be right, World,
or do you want to be happy?

Let's say we're both wrong.

●

Words took the long
weekend off.

"Dreamholes!"

AIN'T NO SHORTY
WEAR THOSE SORRY-ASS
BOWLING SHOES

Woman's bathroom stall,
door closed,
yet she refers to me as *Sir?*

I came here to blow
obeah curses
from wall-mount hair dryers.

Superstition brings nothing
but bad luck
and Officer Devonshire.

X ON THE SCORE SHEET

As long as you're breathing
something should transpire.
Distinguish my body's pulp

from shards of windshield
decorating the road. Our breath's
moisture collected on glass,

forming tiny rivulets
that run together.

●

Chapel's exit: a membrane
one passes through back into
the world. What it filters

is unclear. With no weight
behind words, they dissipate
into air: a hint of rye

the faint mark of their existence.
There are things to say,
but never a way of starting.

We might as well go bowling.

ACKNOWLEDGEMENTS

This book is dedicated to Joan, Jim, and David: the family that came later.

Thanks to the Yukon government's Advanced Artist Award program for a grant that made the writing of *Dazzle Ships* possible.

Thanks, also, to the editors of *Bad Nudes, Bat City Review, Cough, Dusie: Tuesday Poem, The Impressment Gang, Matrix, The Maynard, Our Teeth, PRISM International, The Puritan, Qwerty,* and *Zouch,* for publishing earlier versions of these poems.

JAMIE SHARPE is the author of *Animal Husbandry Today* (ECW, 2012) and *Cut-up Apologetic* (ECW, 2015).